D1572742

Animals
of the World

The
Manatees
of Florida

by Bill Lund

Content Consultant:
Judith Vallee, Executive Director
Save the Manatee Club

Hilltop Books

An Imprint of Franklin Watts
A Division of Grolier Publishing
New York London Hong Kong Sydney
Danbury, Connecticut

Hilltop Books
http://publishing.grolier.com
Copyright © 1998 by Capstone Press • All rights reserved
Published simultaneously in Canada • Printed in the United States of America

Library of Congress Cataloging-in-Publication Data
Lund, Bill, 1954-
    The Manatees of Florida/by Bill Lund.
    p. cm.--(Animals of the world)
    Includes bibliographical references (p. 23).
    Summary: Introduces the world of manatees, their physical characteristics,
behavior, and interaction with humans.
    ISBN 1-56065-579-8
    1. Trichechus manatus--Juvenile literature. [1. Manatees.]
I. Title. II. Series.
QL737.S63L85 1998
599.5'09759--dc21

                                        97-12673
                                          CIP
                                          AC

Photo credits
Innerspace Visions/Doug Perrine, cover, 4, 8, 10, 12, 14, 16, 18-
William Muñoz, 6
Herb Segars, 20

Table of Contents

About Manatees 5
What Manatees Look Like 7
Where Manatees Live 9
What Manatees Do 11
Manatee Enemies and Dangers 13
Mating and Reproduction 15
Newborn and Young Manatees 17
Sirenians 19
Manatees and People 21

Fast Facts 22
Words to Know 23
Read More 23
Useful Addresses 24
Internet Sites 24
Index 24

About Manatees

Manatees are mammals that live in water. A mammal is a warm-blooded animal that has a backbone. Warm-blooded means that an animal's body is always the same temperature. Temperature is how hot or cold something is.

There are three kinds of manatees. These are the Amazonian manatee, the West African manatee, and the West Indian manatee. This book is about West Indian manatees. They live in the waters in and around Florida. They are often called Florida manatees.

Florida manatees are large. The average length of adult male manatees is 10 feet (three meters). Their average weight is 1,000 pounds (450 kilograms). Females are smaller than males.

Manatees spend their lives in water. They eat plants that grow underwater. Manatees are sometimes called sea cows.

Manatees spend their lives in water.

What Manatees Look Like

Florida manatees are gray or grayish-brown. Their skin is thick and wrinkled. A layer of fat under the skin helps keep manatees warm.

Manatees have big heads with small eyes. Their upper lip is split into two halves. Manatees use their upper lips to push plants into their mouths. Whiskers grow on manatees' noses. They also have strong teeth for chewing plants.

Manatees breathe through two small holes on the tops of their noses. These holes are called nostrils. Manatees close their nostrils when they are underwater. They open their nostrils to breathe at the water's surface.

Manatees have tails shaped like paddles. They use these powerful tails for swimming. They also have two small front flippers. Each flipper has three or four claws. Manatees use their flippers to steer and to eat.

Manatees have big heads with small eyes.

Where Manatees Live

Florida manatees live in rivers near the Atlantic Ocean along the coast of Florida. Sometimes they swim in the ocean. In summer, they move farther north.

Florida manatees can live in both fresh water and salt water. Rivers and lakes have fresh water. There is no salt in fresh water. Oceans have salt water. Manatees prefer water warmer than 68 degrees Fahrenheit (20 degrees Celsius).

Manatees live where the water is three to 10 feet (one to three meters) deep. They eat only plants that grow underwater. Plants need sunlight to grow. Sunlight reaches only about 15 feet (four and one-half meters) underwater. Manatees live near places where plants can grow.

Florida manatees may live alone during spring, summer, and fall. In winter, they come together at warmer rivers. Some rivers are warm because of electric power plants. The power plants send warm water into nearby rivers.

Manatees eat only plants that grow underwater.

What Manatees Do

Manatees must eat a lot of food to stay warm. They spend six to eight hours a day eating. They eat up to 100 pounds (45 kilograms) of plants a day. They push plants into their mouths with their flippers and upper lips.

Manatees rest for two to 12 hours a day. They rest at the bottom or near the surface of the water.

Manatees must come to the surface of the water to breathe. This is called surfacing. When they are active, manatees surface every three to five minutes. When resting, they surface about every 20 minutes.

Manatees usually live alone. But they are friendly and playful when they meet other manatees. Manatees seem to kiss and hug when they greet each other. They also chase each other and roll around.

Manatees are gentle animals. They do not attack humans or other animals. Female manatees will not even attack other animals to protect their young.

Manatees seem to hug when they greet each other.

Manatee Enemies and Dangers

Manatees do not have natural enemies. They are safe from many enemies because they live in shallow water. Shallow means not deep. Most animals that could hurt manatees live in deeper water.

The greatest danger to Florida manatees is people. People drive boats in the waters around Florida. Sometimes the boats hit manatees. Many manatees are hurt or killed. Most manatees have marks from accidents with boats. Trash thrown in the water is also harmful to manatees.

People also destroy places where manatees live. People build houses and factories near the ocean and rivers. Factories often put chemicals in the water. Some chemicals kill plants. This means there is less food for the manatees. Chemicals can make manatees sick, too.

Most manatees have marks from accidents with boats.

Mating and Reproduction

Manatees can mate at any time during the year. Mate means to join together to produce young.

Female manatees are called cows. Male manatees are called bulls. Cows can reproduce when they are between four and six years old. Bulls can mate when they are five to nine years old.

Up to 10 bulls follow a cow and try to mate with her. They push each other to try to get near the cow.

The cow mates with several bulls. She gives birth about 13 months after mating. The cow will be ready to mate again in two to three years.

Bulls push each other to try to get near a cow.

Newborn and Young Manatees

A newborn manatee is called a calf. Manatee cows usually give birth to one calf. Sometimes cows give birth to two calves. A calf is about three feet (one meter) long at birth. It weighs 60 to 70 pounds (27 to 31 kilograms).

A calf stays very close to its mother. It drinks milk from her body. The cow teaches her calf how to surface so it can breathe. She also teaches it how to find food and warm water. The calf begins eating plants a few weeks after birth.

Cows and calves play together. They make squeaking and squealing sounds. This helps cows know where their calves are at all times.

Cows take care of their calves. But calves are ready to live on their own after about two years.

A calf drinks milk from a cow's body.

Sirenians

Florida manatees belong to a group of mammals called sirenians. Sirenians live in water and eat only plants. The Amazonian manatee and the West African manatee are also sirenians.

Another animal called the dugong belongs to the sirenian group. Dugongs look a lot like manatees, but they are smaller. Their tails are less rounded than manatees' tails. Each dugong has two long teeth that stick out of its mouth.

Dugongs live along the coasts of east Africa, Asia, New Guinea, and Australia. Unlike manatees, dugongs live only in salt water. They stay in the ocean all the time.

There was once another sirenian called the Steller's sea cow. In the 1700s, hunters killed these sea cows for their meat. By 1771, Steller's sea cows had become extinct. Extinct means no longer living anywhere in the world.

Florida manatees belong to a group of mammals called sirenians.

Manatees and People

Scientists believe there are fewer than 3,000 Florida manatees alive today. Hunting, boating, and other problems have made manatees an endangered species. Endangered means in danger of becoming extinct. Species means a kind of animal.

Many people work to save the manatees. The state of Florida made a law in 1978. The law says that Florida is a sanctuary for manatees. A sanctuary is a safe place. Boats must travel at slow speeds where manatees live. It is against the law to kill or hurt manatees.

People can see and learn about Florida manatees. Manatees live in Florida zoos. People can watch manatees near some power plants.

Many programs help manatees. People study manatees to learn more about them. People also help sick or hurt manatees. Florida manatees need humans to help protect them.

People study manatees to learn more about them.

Fast Facts

Common Name: Florida manatee

Scientific name: Trichechus manatus

Life span: Not known if wild; 60 to 70 years in zoos.

Length: Adult male manatees are 10 feet (three meters) long. Females are a little shorter.

Weight: Adult male manatees average 1,000 pounds (450 kilograms). Females weigh less.

Features: Manatees have thick gray or grayish-brown skin. They have big heads with whiskers and small eyes. They have tails shaped like paddles and two small front flippers.

Population: There are about 3,000 Florida manatees.

Home: Florida manatees live in rivers near the Atlantic Ocean along the coast of Florida. Sometimes they swim in the ocean.

Habits: Florida manatees spend their lives in shallow parts of the ocean and rivers. They spend six to eight hours a day eating. Adults usually live alone except when mating or caring for young.

Diet: Florida manatees eat plants that grow in Florida rivers and the Atlantic Ocean.

Words to Know

endangered species (en-DAYN-jurd SPEE-sheez)—a kind of animal in danger of becoming extinct

extinct (ehk-STINKT)—no longer living anywhere in the world

mammal (MAM-uhl)—a warm-blooded animal that has a backbone; baby mammals drink milk from their mothers' bodies

mate (MAIT)—to join together to produce young

sanctuary (SANGK-choo-er-ee)—a safe place

sirenians (sih-REH-nee-uhnz)—a group of mammals that live in water, including manatees and dugongs

surfacing (SUR-fiss-ing)—coming to the surface of the water to breathe

Read More

Clark, Margaret Goff. *The Vanishing Manatee*. New York: Dutton, 1990.

Greene, Carol. *Reading About the Manatee*. Hillside, N.J.: Enslow, 1993.

Useful Addresses

Sea World of Florida
Education Department
7007 Sea World Drive
Orlando, FL 32809

Florida Audubon Society
1101 Audubon Way
Maitland, FL 32751

Internet Sites

Save the Manatee Club
http://www.objectlinks.com/manatee

Manatee Junction
http://ourworld.compuserve.com/homepages/shannonc/
index.htm

Index

Amazonian manatee, 5, 19
bull, 15
calf, 17
cow, 15, 17
dugong, 19
endangered species, 21
flipper, 7, 11, 22
mammal, 5, 19

nostrils, 7
plants, 9, 11, 13, 17, 22
sanctuary, 21
sea cows, 5, 19
sirenians, 19
surface, 11, 17
West African manatee, 5, 19
West Indian manatee, 5